Happy Hauntings

By Jacqueline James

Published by Parables   August, 2020

All Rights Reserved. No part of this book may be reproduced or utilized in any form or by any means, electronic or mechanical, including photocopying, recording, or by any information storage and retrieval system, without the permission in writing from the author.

Readers should be aware that Internet Web sites offered as citations and/or sources for further information may have been changed or disappeared between the time this was written and when it is read.

ISBN   978-1-951497-86-6   Copyright by Jacqueline James

Happy Hauntings

By Jacqueline James
Illustrated by Davonne Newell

Table of Contents

A Scary Night 2

A Gigantic Black Hole … 4

Mean Monstrous Machine… 6

Blank Face… 8

The Crooked Cat… 10

Icy Mountains… 12

Three Spooky Red Houses… 14

Old Pine Tree… 16

Under the Rug… 18

Darken Camp Fire … 20

Raindrops of Blood … 22

Ghostly Shadows … 24

The Beat of Doom … 26

The Upside-Down Bed… 28

The Empty Wagon... 30

The Backyard Dog… 32

No Rain… 34

Tiny House of Horror … 36

12 Bullfrogs … 38

Scary Things … 40

Aqua Blue Pool … 42

Haunted Horn of Horror … 44

Table of Contents (cont.)

The Garage Door … 46
The Spooky Dinner Diner … 48
Pumpkin Eater Yum Yum Yum… 50
The Dead Eye Fish … 52
The Scary Man … 54
12 to 1 Ravens … 56
Fear That Smell … 58
Hey Piggy-Piggy … 60
The Backyard … 62
About the Author..64

A Scary Night …

It was a dark and cold scary night
When all the town lost their light
The towns' people all started to wonder
Why darkness crept through every corner
The children cried because they
were scared
By the creepy sounds that were heard
But when their mothers tried to calm
them down
They too shook and trembled from
the sound
Now all the fathers big and brave
Stepped right up to save the day
They gathered up the brightest lights
Then went outside into the night
They walked slowly down the scary street
Not knowing what they were going to meet
What they saw made them scream
From the scary, spooky, darken scene
There were hundreds of black cats
all around
Covering the street of their small town
So they shined their lights until they went dim
Which made the cats jump onto tree limbs
'Cause the brightness scared each
one of them
Then the fathers quickly returned home
Never knowing what went wrong.

A Gigantic Black Hole …

It was a very scary terrifying day
When the land decided to give way
A gigantic black hold sunk through the earth
And it took four houses and eight cars
for its thirst
It sunk in deep with a crushing sound
And uprooted trees from the ground
In two of the cars were baby car seats
And on the dining room table was good
food to eat
All of the cars had nice stereos
And each of the houses had new
carpeted floors
There were beautiful kid's rooms
but no children around
And there were parent rooms but no
mommies to be found
Luckily for them all they weren't at home
Or else they would've been trapped inside
the sinkhole
Those who actually saw the disturbing sight
Stood shaking and shivering filled with fright
"What if that was I?" One of the viewers asked.
Then someone responded "there'd be none of
you left."

Mean Monstrous Machine…

It was a spooky silver and gray
mean monstrous machine
A ghostly vehicle that came on the scene
It spooked its viewers passing by
Some were so scared they started
to cry
It was covered with spikes and
skeleton heads
And blood dripping from its tire treads
Its windows were tinted very dark
And it sparked a flame when it
parked
Then several spectators started to scream
Some said that nightmares haunted their
dreams
Others waited with caution for the doors
to open
Only to find a scary goblin
Their hearts skipped a beat from what
they saw
One could only imagine the fear in them all
While some fainted others ran
But it was just a spooky costume
worn by a skinny old man.

Blank Face…

There was a girl who took a dare
To go into an old house to find ghost anywhere
However she didn't come out the same way she went in
Cause she was frightened from within
There was no expression on her face
As she came racing through the dark and spooky place
The ghostly figures frightened her
And left her with a blank stare
She was struck with shock by what she saw
As if her face was stuck in 'AWE'
I heard there was blood and guts everywhere
And the smell of death was in the air
It was a horrible haunted dreadful scene
She was scared but she couldn't scream
The place was an old house with goblins and ghosts
And scary decorations by children doing the most
She only went in because she was pressured
But she left the place with no expression.

The Crooked Cat…

There was a crooked cat with lots of
crooked curves
If you look too long you'll lose
your nerves
Everyone who stopped and stared
at him
Left quickly shaking, swamped with
fear
Rumors rang out he was covered
with stitch
All tangled up from a ragweed ditch
One man got the courage to pull
them off,
But the cat started squealing from his
mouth
So the man changed his mind
And didn't pull the thorns from the
cat's spine
He left the crooked cat all
tangled up
With vines and weeds coming from
his gut.

Icy Mountains…

There were icy cold mountains over a black valley below
As far as the eyes could see it was covered with snow
Rumors were of a ghost that haunted the land
Tall and spooky with a shovel for a hand
He creeps through the night leaving his footsteps in the snow
He makes horrible screeching noises wherever he goes
The sound echoes from the mountains then roars through the valley
Keeping everyone whispering about the story I'm telling
When the morning had come and the footprints were found
Many nervous spectators gathered around
All of them wondered, "What were the spooky night sounds?"
But a path of snow was shoved from the icy ground.

Three Spooky Red Houses…

Three spooky red houses on the block
People walked pass but dare not stop
I just heard someone who said
That blood dripping from the house roof is what made them red
Each house was completely red as far as I know
Red covered the windows and the grass below
Dark was the color of the shade
With ghostly figures as if they were made
Wherever darkness forms around
Spooky shadows circle the ground
Scary loud crashes and bumps were the sounds,
And in the morning empty buckets were found.
The neighbors saw this as a threat to them all
But I saw it as a paint job gone very wrong.

Old Pine Tree...

I was on my way to sleep late
one night
But what I saw through my window
was quite a fright
It was a rugged old beat up pine tree
That looked as if it was staring at me
The autumn wind blew its branches
closer to my window
The black ghostly shadow is what I
remember
As they hit against my window pane
The sound of terror nearly drove me insane
I grabbed my covers to hide my head
Then sunk deeper and deeper into my bed
The branches hit strongly against
my house
One cracked the glass window but I
couldn't open my mouth
I wanted to scream but I was shocked
in fear
I felt the presence of the tree
being near
The old tree uprooted from the ground
Spooky images formed around
I took a peek from under the cover
Then came the light and there was
no longer.

Under the Rug…

In the basement and under a rug,
There was a photo of a ghost who
needed a hug
On the photo his arms stretched
out wide
And if you took one peep
you would be trapped inside
The more who looked the photo
grew larger
But no one know how to get them out of
the horror
Those who lifted the rug not
paying attention were never seen
again just reported missing
A decision was made to tear down
the house,
But first things needed to be
moved out.
The mover discovered a secret
door.
When they lifted the rug from the
floor
There were some very steep steps
leading down to the cellar
And was it hundreds of people
down there yelling.

Darken Camp Fire …

Around the campfire, dark and grim
Something white was glowing from within
It sparked a twinkle of light
That spread some mysteries through the night
The campers wondered, "What could it be?"
The ghostly glow that they all had seen
The light that flickered through the fire
Showered them all with a spooky awe
Suddenly after the fire was gone
The midnight darkness fell upon
Then all the campers began to scream
From the horribly soaking darken scene
A storm had flooded their campground
And put out the fire that was burning wild.

Raindrops of Blood …

One haunted day rain drops of
blood covered the ground
Each drop splashed with a deadly
sound
It soaked the yards onto the curves
Those who stood and watched had
some ghostly nerves
It splattered on the trees and onto
the rooftops
Then dripped down the side of
everyone's house
It flooded the streets and clogged the
sewer drains
This horrible blood came from
clouds of rains
Someone even noticed a blood
soaked man
Panicking horribly with an umbrella
in his hand
They all desperately wondered where it
came from
So they looked to the clouds
for an answer from above
Turns out a plane carrying a red
paint tank burst in the air
Which dripped through the clouds
and the wind sprayed it everywhere.

Ghostly Shadows …

Ghostly shadows were seen late one afternoon
Then an eerie silence covered the room
The curtains had been drawn in the kitchen area
And spooky images entered which were quite scary
Mama was in the kitchen washing dishes
Then she was haunted by a
vision she dared not mention
Her eyes bucked and she became weak
She couldn't move nor could she speak
Then daddy entered the room shortly afterwards
And he was horrified to find a
ghostly shadow
So he left the room walking backwards
Then sister entered shortly afterwards
She saw the same image creeping past
And she ran out the room very fast
Finally the brother came in when he heard the sound
He looked around and began to frown
He said, "Really you all don't know?
It's just the way the wind is
blowing the hung out clothes.

The Beat of Doom …

BOOM! BOOM! BOOM!
Was the beat of doom
That could be heard for miles one
afternoon
BOOM! BOOM! BOOM!
The sound grew louder
Surrounded by terror that soon
followed
Everyone in the room was struck
with panic
As the spooky sound behind a door grew
even louder
And before long the room was
cleared
Because of the frightened noises that
they heard
Only a few brave ones stayed
behind
Determined to see what they would find
They couldn't bare the noise anymore
So they crept in closer to the door
Then their hearts raced and their knees
got weaker
Only to discover a baby boy hitting
a wood spoon against a speaker.

The Upside-Down Bed…

There was once an upside down bed
If you laid on it, it'll flip your head
Your toes will be at the top and your
head will be at the bottom
And if you laid too long you'll begin
to holla
The mattress will flip upside down
Then your face will point right to the
ground
If you don't hold on tight you'll hit
the floor
And won't ever lay in that bed no more
I was once asked to make that bed
But I didn't know which end to lay
the spread
If I'd laid it at the top it would be
upside down
But if I laid it at the bottom it would
spin itself around
So I just decided to put it in the middle
And let someone else solve the riddle.

The Empty Wagon...

Eight horses were trotting up a hill
Pulling an empty wagon heading
toward the mills
An empty wagon that was full
Filled with ghosts and spooky tales
All that heard the ghostly sounds
Knew the empty wagon was coming
around
People near began to worry
They dread to hear the deadly
stories
The further the wagon the closer
they got
No one knew what that was about
When the wagon was coming near
They saw the sound of a ghost
appear
But when it approached it was
nothing there
Only ghostly sounds haunted the
atmosphere
Some searched the wagon for
the noise
Only to find a recorded toy.

The Backyard Dog…

I went to visit a friend late one evening
He said come quickly because he was leaving
But the front door was blocked and I couldn't get in
I went to the backyard to meet my friend
But in the backyard was a vicious dog
This dog was mean and it was not small
Before I touched the gate the dog started to bark
Then all I saw was large white canines shining in the dark
I got so frightened until I lost my balance
But the dog started growling while I was yelling
I said, "Help me, come out and get your dog.
This dog trying to bite me! What's going on?"
Then my friend looked out the window from his home
And said, 'that ain't my dog you on your own!'

No Rain…

The darkness fell upon the sky
But no one could explain the reason why
When the clouds formed everyone was expecting rain
But the dark skies were all they gained
The sky gave dark clouds but no rain came
Those who stared nearly went insane
As the clouds spread wider the darkness went darker
Others glanced quickly because they were smarter
It was late that evening as the sun went down
And blackened silence covered the ground
The dark clouds brought thoughts of rain showers
So everyone ran to take cover
But the wind blew hard and still no rain
The day grew near but the darkness remained
The people were nervous and became alarmed
Then all of a sudden fell a terrible rainstorm.

Tiny House of Horror …

It was a tiny house of horror, built for two
That reeked terror only on a few
Everyone who occupied this tiny space
Left quickly with horror plastered on their face
Rumors were the house folded up
Leaving a couple trapped inside when it shut
For hours you could their deadly screams
Until eventually rescuers came on the scene
They pried open the house with a
reckoning team
But it left the occupants with nightmares
that haunted their dreams
The next tenants that came to stay the night
Was awakened at 3 am by quite a fright
Their hearts were pounding through
their skin
When they felt the house closing
from within
Panic set in, then they began to shout
But luckily for them they managed to get out
Now they would have a horrible tale to tell
That house is haunted this they yelled
The realtors who heard them say all of that
Said the house wasn't finished and
that's a fact
They should have rented not even to a few
Before the final construction was
completely through.

12 Bullfrogs …

One horrible night in the darken fog
You can hear the sound of 12
bullfrogs
They hop back and forth in the streets
Making squeaky noises with their feet
Everyone who tried to walk pass
The frogs stopped them quickly in
their path
Some leaped and jumped on their backs
They were so scary it made the
people sweat
One old man dropped his hat
But he ran so fast and didn't look back
I heard a lady dropped her purse
She was so scared she began to curse
One little boy who got to close
Trying to catch the frogs doing the most
He reached to grab one with his hand
But when the frog leaped forward
the boy peed his pants
Then a little girl came and made a bet
And out of her pocket she pulled a net
She caught a frog when she tried her best
Then she said, "Don't be scared I'll catch the rest."

Scary Things …

If you're in the streets at a quarter to
nine
There's some scary things that you will find
It's an old lady with a patch on her eye
She'll take your candy but I don't know
why
She'll snatch your bag with all your stuff
Then close your mouth and tape it shut
She'll drag you into her spooky house
Then put you in a cellar with a
rotten mouse
She'll leave you there for two whole hours
You'll lose your manners and need
a shower
You'll be so scared you'll scream out loud
But with the tape you can't make a sound
She'll pull you out by your stinky clothes
All the while holding her nose
Then she'll open her door and you'll
run out fast
And never ever mention the past.

Aqua Blue Pool …

At the deep end of the aqua blue pool
There's an energy that will suck you into its gravity being rude
If you're in the water floating or swimming
This force will pull you to its very middle
It you try to hold on the pool walls
The force will grab you and make you fall
Once it compels you in there's no getting out
You'll circle for hours around and about
The powerful possession will keep you there
If you want to leave out it doesn't care
You'll fight and struggle with lots of splash
While others I the pool will swim on passed
They'll hear the swooshy, squishy sounds flooding the room
Coming through the jets of the whirlpools.

Haunted Horn of Horror …

It was a haunted horn of horror
That only played bad news
If you heard the evil noise
It was close to somebody's doom
The sounds were very loud
And they'll get stuck inside your head
It was the haunted horn of horror
That everyone seemed to dread
On one horrible blackened afternoon
The sound of fatality flooded the room
Soon to follow was an eerie silence
That ran away several scary cowards
Those that stayed were the ones that were brave
To witness the sounds of the "Green Beret."

The Garage Door …

I heard a horrible crash from my garage door
When it slammed itself shut unto the floor
Followed by spooky noises all around
I stopped what I was doing and ran toward the sound
But there wasn't a single person to be found
Only large black footprints on the ground
I went for a mop to get them up
But when I returned the garage door was up
I took a peep outside the yard
And saw a ghostly figure scary and large
But before I could process it all
The garage door slammed back down
This time I got locked out
And heard strange noises moving on the side of my house
At that point I took off and ran
Then bumped right into the maintenance man.

The Spooky Dinner Diner …

We were at a dinner late one
evening
And it was unbelievable the things we
were seeing
Most of the people were at an awe
From the spooky things that they saw
I, on the other hand, wasn't
bothered at all
So I took out my phone and made a call
I invited my friends to all come around
To view the scary sights and hear the
spooky sounds
Then I used my phone to take a picture
But when I tried to send it the image
was missing
So I tried again but it was spooky
and strange
Cause the screen was blank just
the same
Now I wasn't so brave anymore
So I ran and met my friends at the
door.

Pumpkin Eater Yum Yum Yum…

"Pumpkin eater, pumpkin eater YUM YUM YUM
Chewing on you is better than gum!"
Were the scary chants heard from afar
Spooky sounds which were very bizarre
You could hear the chatter from every room
Going back and forth one rainy afternoon
"Pumpkin eater pumpkin eater YUM YUM YUM
Chewing on you is lots of fun!"
The sounds grew close then moved far away
The haunting noises spooked our day
We looked in and out of every room
Then we went outside to follow the noise of doom
We tried our best to find the sounds
But no one visible was ever found.

The Dead Eye Fish ...

It was a dead eye fish served at the table
Baked with onion from someone's labor
The fish was placed on a plate
Only to be eaten was its 'steak'
The chef decided to leave on the head
The eyes were open but the fish was dead
Those who looked into the eyes were bold
Cause the fish could see inside their soul
One could see that the fish eyes were black
But they never saw their reflections back
What they did see chilled their bones
Which left them scared to be alone
They later had horrible things to say
How the fish had stared their souls away
But the chef called it a gourmet dish
Known as the 'baked blackened dead eye fish.'

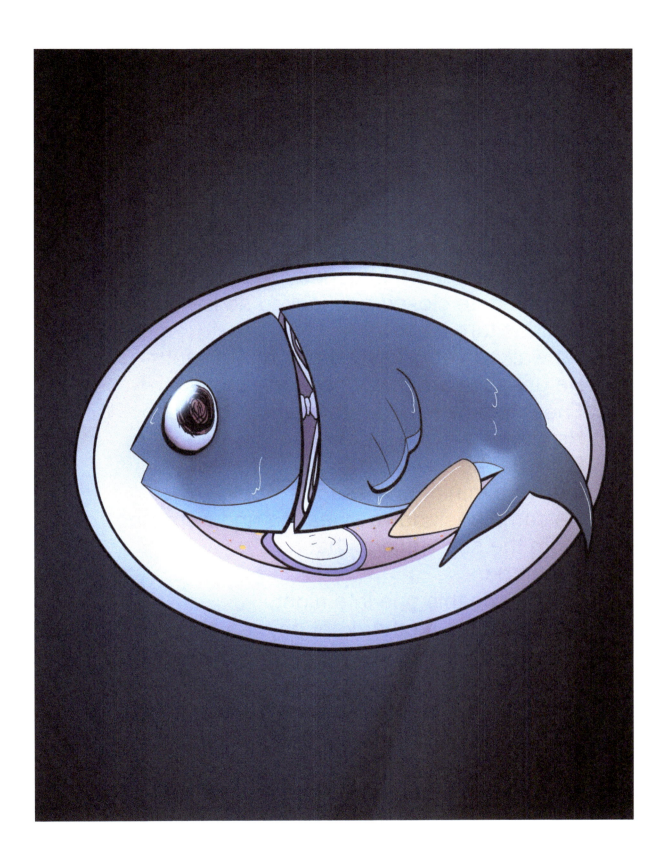

The Scary Man …

Up the ladder onto the roof
There's a scary old man with a hoof for his foot
He walks with a limp and he uses a cane
All that racket will drive you insane
I heard this from a neighborhood boy
Who had the nerves to go into his yard
He was so scared because it was all pitch black
But the gate closed and locked so he
couldn't turn back
He walked very slowly dragging his feet
He got so scared until he started to weep
Then he saw a ladder that was very steep
He climbed to the top then took a peep
But what he saw next made him weak
It gave him nightmares for a week
He came back down sweating and trembling
From the scary things that he
remembers
He told me this one late night
And insist his mother kept on the lights
He said since the visit he hasn't been right
Ever since he saw that scary site
He said your ears will ring with fear
And you will shake and tremble
from the things you hear
If you go up that ladder and see that man
Holding his hook foot in his hand.

12 to 1 Ravens …

Down in the valley up at the top of a hill
There sat 12 ravens who decided to chill
The first raven called out to the
raven sitting next to him
Here comes two people so let's scare them
So they both flapped their wings
and flew down low
To spook the pedestrians walking below
The first raven perched on the
youngest shoulder
While the other raven landed on the
back of the oldest
When the two people attempted to
take off and run
Two more ravens flew down for fun
One person panicked and his
mouth just hung
The other eight ravens were soon awaken
And flew down to join the
racket they were making
All twelve of the ravens circled their head
One person fainted and the other
person said
"Ravens only come when someone
is dead."

Fear That Smell …

Something must have crawled up in you and died
Because you were smelling so foul I almost lost my mind
I felt threatened when you came near
Your horrible odor flushed me with fear
The odor dominated the atmosphere
While it's rotten scent polluted my breathing air
Once that smell went down my throat
I gagged, coughed and then I choked
I couldn't imagine that the odor came from you
I thought it was something that the witches had brew
The smell grew stronger when you walked pass
Then you excused yourself because you just had gas.

Hey Piggy-Piggy …

One spooky night on Halloween
I came upon a ghostly scene
I spotted four piggy's digging hard
In the middle of a darkened graveyard
So I decided to call out loud
Hoping for my words to move the crowd
"Hey piggy-piggy what you digging?
Is that a corpse from some ones bones?
Can you leave them to rot on their own?"
They were in a graveyard dark and black
Hoofing and scratching and
wouldn't turn back
So I called out to them once again
Hoping that they would comprehend
"Hey piggy-piggy stop digging them bones!
Leave them graves, now go ahead on!"
But they turned to me then scratched their hoofs
And continue to dig the graves real rough
Then up popped some bones from the grave
Those were the ones I could not save
Then amongst the pigs they began to fight
Over the bones they dug up that night
"Hey piggy-piggy what are you doing,
With them bones that you just ruined?"
They turned towards me as if they dared,
But I took off running cause I got scared.

The Backyard …

The vacant house with the big backyard
Trying to walk through is going to
be hard
Cause it's filled with rubbish, bottles
and sticks
Dry rotten tires and broken glass
Old raggedy clothes and sewer rats
The chase is on for all stray cats
There's large tree limbs that have
fallen down
And unraked leaves on the ground
"Oh my goodness something's
smelling bad!
There's a year's word of unemptied
trash."
There's an old garage that's stale
and musty
Filled with copper pipes that are cracked
and rusty
There's weeds and brushes growing
all around
And dead rodents covering the
ground
There's cracked concrete with large
pot holes
With no sign of life not even a mole
The entrance gate is falling apart
So if I were you I wouldn't go there in the dark.

About the Author

Happy Haunting is a children's book of 31 spooky poems written for children to enjoy over the Halloween season. The intention is to 'happily' haunt each household every Halloween with our ghostly poems and images.

Written by five star poetess:

Jacqueline James

To read other inspiring books by the author please visit the website

rhymes64.weebly.com

Book illustrations by talented 8th grade Artist:

Davonne Newell

Her specialty is both digital and sketch artwork.

IG@dweeby.creates

Published by Parables

Printed in the USA
CPSIA information can be obtained
at www.ICGtesting.com
CBHW080159010724
10738CB00004B/38